THE WAITING ROOM, 1856
From a drawing by W. McConnell in THE TRAIN

Lewis Carroll, born January 27, 1832
A Centenary Tribute

Fig. 1: Lewis Caroll, Aged 23

FOR THE TRAIN

FIVE POEMS AND A TALE
BY
LEWIS CARROLL

Being Contributions to "The Train," 1856-1857, with the original illustrations by C. H. Bennett and W. McConnell; together with some Carrollean Episodes concerning Trains

Arranged, with a Preface, by

HUGH J. SCHONFIELD

Author of "Letters to Frederick Tennyson," etc.

Originally published by

DENIS ARCHER

6 Old Gloucester Street W.C.1

January, 1932

Second Impression February, 1932

Reset and edited ©2022 Stephen Engelking

Texianer Verlag for the Hugh and Helene Schonfield World Service Trust

ISBN: 978-3-949197-91-8

TO MARION, WHOSE MOTHER WAS ONCE THE MARCH HARE

THE
TRAIN:
A First-Class Magazine

"VIRES ACQIRIT EUNDO"

VOL I.—FROM JANUARY TO JUNE, 1856.

LONDON:

GROOMBRIDGE AND SONS, PATERNOSTER ROW.

MDCCCLVI.

[*The Authors of Articles in* "THE TRAIN," *reserve to themselves the right of Translation.*]
TITLE PAGE TO THE TRAIN, VOLUME I.

CONTENTS

Preface	11
PROLOGUE	21
THE PATH OF ROSES	31
THE THREE VOICES	39
THE SAILOR'S WIFE	53
HIAWATHA'S PHOTOGRAPHING	59
NOVELTY AND ROMANCEMENT	67
SOME CARROLLEAN EPISODES CONCERNING TRAINS	83

LIST OF ILLUSTRATIONS

The Waiting Room, 1856 *(From a drawing by W. McConell)*	1
Lewis Caroll, Aged 23 *(From a photograph)*	2
Title Page to THE TRAIN	6
Illustration to *Solitude* *(From a drawing by W. McConell)*	27
Illustration to *The Path of Roses* *(From a drawing by C. H. Bennett)*	33
Illustration to *The Sailor's Wife* *(From a drawing by C. H. Bennett)*	55
Illustration to *Novelty and Romancement*	81
Illustration to *Through the Looking Glass* *(From a drawing by Sir John Tenniel)*	87
Illustration to *Sylvie and Bruno* *(From a drawing by Harry Furniss)*	92

PREFACE

BY

Hugh J. Schonfield

IF other justification for this small volume be needed, than the desire to mark the centenary of the birth of Lewis Carroll with some small tribute to his genius, it may be found in the nature of the material selected for the purpose.

I am of the opinion, which the sales of this book will either confirm or disprove, that a collection for the first time of all Lewis Carroll's contributions to The Train will be acceptable to his many admirers, especially as it was in this magazine that the famous nom de plume first appeared in print, at the head of the poem entitled Solitude, published in the March No. of Volume I. Mr. Langford Reed, in a recent Centenary Appreciation of Carroll,[*] has repeated the error that it was a later poem The Path of Roses which held this distinction, and the same author has unaccountably dated The Train 1861, instead of 1856.

The story of how the Reverend Charles Lutwidge Dodgson came to adopt the pseudonym[†] of Lewis Carroll

---

[*] Supplement to John O' London's Weekly, December, 1931.
[†] The Life and Letters of Lewis Carroll, 1898, p. 67.

has been well told by his biographer S. Dodgson Collingwood,* but it may be suitably repeated here. The young author first suggested "Dares" (the first syllable of his birthplace, Daresbury) to Edmund Yates, editor of The Train, "but, as this did not meet with his editor's approval, he wrote again, giving a choice of four names: (1) Edgar Cuthwellis, (2) Edgar U. C. Westhall, (3) Louis Carroll, and (4) Lewis Carroll. The first two were formed from the letters of his two Christian names, Charles Lutwidge; the others are merely variant forms of those names—Lewis = Ludovicus = Lutwidge; Carroll = Carolus = Charles." Yates chose the last of these, and we cannot doubt that the choice was a happy one.

History does not relate whether The Train, which was a monthly publication, was particularly intended for the delectation of railway travellers, but for the purposes of this book that has been assumed to be the case. The magazine came into existence in 1856 as a result of the sale of *The Comic Times*, founded in 1853 by the proprietor of *The Illustrated News*, the whole staff leaving and starting the new venture on the change of ownership, when *The Comic Times* was reduced to half its size. Edmund Yates, editor of the former periodical, became the enthusiastic conductor of THE TRAIN, and in this he was ably assisted by George Augustus Sala and Frank Smedley. It was through Smedley that Mr. Dodgson became a contributor to *The Comic Times*, and Yates had expressed warm approval of his efforts. It was natural, therefore, that he should write for the new magazine.

The Scene, printed in the first number of THE TRAIN, from which I have taken some passages to form a Prologue, shows us what a happy company of contributors were assembled to give the magazine a royal send off. Originally issued by the well-known firm of Groombridge & Sons, it was later transferred to Beeton's in Bouverie Street; but, alas, after four volumes had been published it reached its "terminus."

During the two years, 1856-57, Carroll contributed to THE TRAIN five poems: *Solitude* (March, 1856); *The Path of Roses* (May, 1856); *The Three Voices* (November, 1856); *The Sailor's Wife* (May, 1857); *Hiawatha's Photographing* (December, 1857); and a tale *Novelty and Romancement* (October, 1856). All of these, except the tale, have since been included in published collections of Carroll's poems, such as *Rhyme and Reason*, Macmillan, 1883, and *Three Sunsets*, Macmillan, 1898, but never as a group by themselves, or with the original illustrations of C. H. Bennett and W. McConnell.

The poems are not very meritorious, judged by poetic standards, but the author's age—he was only twenty-four—must be taken into consideration. They do, however, reveal both the serious and the comic side of his character, which were so fascinatingly blended throughout his life.

Solitude is a reverie filled with that sadness and regretfulness which imaginative youth is so prone to credit to old age.

The Path of Roses has for its subject "woman's mission," and Dodgson Collingwood describes the lines commencing:

"In the darkest path of man's despair,"

as "full of the noblest chivalry, reminding one of Tennyson's *Idylls of the King*." Certainly, Carroll had long been an admirer of Tennyson's writings, and he met the poet in 1857, and it is possible that he owed something to his inspiration, although the date is too early for the Idylls to have been the source.

The unnamed heroine of The Path of Roses is evidently Florence Nightingale:

> "But there was one that ever, to and fro,
> Moved with light footfall; purely calm her face,
> And those deep steadfast eyes that starred the gloom: Still as she went, she ministered to each Comfort and counsel; cooled the fevered brow
> With softest touch, and in the listening ear
> Of the pale sufferer whispered words of peace.
> The dying warrior, gazing as she passed,
> Clasped his thin hands and blessed her."

The Crimean War was but lately ended, and the heroism of the Lady of the Lamp was on everybody's lips. What makes the identification more certain is a clear reference in the same poem to the charge of the Light Brigade at Balaclava.

If Tennyson did not influence *The Path of Roses*, it is likely enough that his *Princess* gave Carroll his theme "For the rather tedious semi-humorous poem *The Three Voices*. The female blue-stocking is here the butt of his wit, and probably the interminable length of the poem is intentional; for the male victim wonders

> "why he had so long preferred
> To hang upon her every word,
> ' In truth,' he said, ' it was absurd.'"

The Sailor's Wife is a dramatic poem in the vein of The Ancient Mariner.

Hiawatha's Photographing delightfully parodies Longfellow's famous poem, even Carroll's introductory note is written in the same metre. Of all the poems, this one probably gave the author the greatest pleasure, as photography was his chief hobby, and he never lost an opportunity of adding a new scalp to his collection, especially if that scalp surmounted the head of a notability.

I have treated these poems of Lewis Carroll so frankly that reviewers will have ample material for their criticisms. I make them a present of the information, and accept their thanks, as I give them mine, in anticipation.

With regard to *Novelty and Romancement*, what can one say of the disillusionment of the redoubtable Mr. Stubbs; he at least did not share the fate of the unfortunate Nosmo King, whose mother by a similar oversight saddled her son with a name which must ever have given him a twinge of conscience when he visited a tobacconist.

FOR THE TRAIN would hardly have been complete without some reference to Lewis Carroll's interest in railway travelling, which was the wonder of the nineteenth century; and it was only when 1 began to go systematically through his books with the object of noting such references that I realised how rich these were. Apart from his skill in recording what he saw and heard, he always looked at the workaday world with the child's mind of wonder and eager curiosity, and, I am accordingly under great obligation to the author's representatives and to Messrs. Macmillan, the publishers, for permission to illustrate this particular appeal of the Train by such lengthy extracts. These I have arranged as far as possible in chronological order, although I can make no claim to completeness, but together with some of the illustrations in the book they do help to convey a certain impression of the progress of the Iron Horse during Lewis Carroll's lifetime. I can only hope that the volume may assist some modern railway-traveller to pass the time as pleasantly as the author whose work it contains would have desired.

In conclusion I wish to express my indebtedness to Messrs. Ernest Benn for permission to use the portrait and extracts from *The Life and Letters of Lewis Carroll*, by S. Dodgson Collingwood, originally published by T. Fisher Unwin, and further to Messrs. Macmillan for the same courtesy with regard to the plates from *Through the Looking Glass* and *Sylvie and Bruno*.

Hugh J. Schonfield.

PROLOGUE

SCENE.—*A Snuggery, nearly filled by a large round table and a small cottage piano. The remaining space is occupied by a dumb-waiter and the persons of various contributors to* THE TRAIN *Monthly Magazine, who are discovered carousing.*

THE EDITOR. Gentlemen, oblige me with a silence in which you could hear a pun drop. Our friend Macaire is about to give us his *Song of the Train*. [*Mr. Macaire takes his seat at the piano, with great alacrity, and preludizes. A dead silence.*

A SARCASTIC CONTRIBUTOR IN RED WHISKERS (*quietly*). I hope it will be something nice and clever about our "Whistle at starting": "Terminus, No. 5, Paternoster-row"; "Traffic-master Mr. Groombridge"; "Tickets, one shilling," and so on, because I am fond of beautiful imagery in poetry.

EDITOR. Will the nearest Ajax have the kindness to beat that Thersites into goodliness. Mr. Macaire, we are all attention.

The Song of the Train

"Harness me down with your iron bands,
  Make sure of your curb and rein,"
But I'll snap the pens in your puny hands
That would stop the wheels of the Train!
  With logs of wood to upset me, try,
    From the skulls of blockheads cleft.
Scrunch! they go—sticks, stones, let fly—
    But behind in scorn they're left.

  The steam is up and away we go!
    On a road that's bright and new;
  Old coach proprietors, heavy and slow,
    Our course with anguish view.
  Meetings they call, and bills they print,
    And their feeble voices strain:
  "Travel with us, nor your life's term stint,
  By that murderous, headlong Train."

  The steam is up and away we go!
    There's a frowning mountain side—
  Never its mysteries man might know—
    Into its heart we ride!
  Here is a yawning valley of death,
    Venture across it not—
No one has dared! in a whistle and breath,
    We are over it like a shot.

> The steam is up and away we go!
> Through vales and pastures green;
> By the old roundabout turnpikes slow
> Ne'er had these lands been seen.
> Hamlets, villages, cities, seas,
> Sever'd as by a wall,
> May sing to each other like birds on trees,
> For the Train unites them all.

[Applause.

EDITOR. Mr. Macaire, your health!

[It is drunk enthusiastically. A pause.

THE SARCASTIC CONTRIBUTOR (*with a sigh*). I wish he had alluded to the stokers by name, and mentioned that extra luggage would be charged for, with a clause against the issue of return tickets.

EDITOR. Gentlemen—THE TRAIN! It will succeed and it shall succeed. It shall sell enormously. There shall not be a bad debt in its ledger any more than a bad line in its pages. It shall keep us all in perennial health and spirits. Such of us as are single shall marry, and such as are married shall be happy. We will grow in wit, and worth, and sense, unheeding critic's pen, and that proverbially vexatious lack of pence shall not trouble us.

Excelsior! There's a good time coming. Gentlemen—
THE TRAIN!

ALL. THE TRAIN! THE TRAIN!*

---

* The scene from which the above passages are excerpted appeared in the first number of The Train under the title of Nights at the Round Table. It is not known whether Lewis Carroll is included among the contributors present who take part in the Dialogue, but it is just possible that one described as "An Amazed Contributor," subsequently addressed by the pseudonym of Quarll, and who is evidently a Varsity man, may be intended for our author; in which case we may suppose that Quarll is a thin disguise for Carroll.—Ed.

SOLITUDE

SOLITUDE

I love the stillness of the wood,
I love the music of the rill,
I love to couch in pensive mood
    Upon some silent hill.

Far off, beneath yon arching trees,
The silver-crested ripples pass,
And, like a mimic brook, the breeze
Whispers among the grass.

Here from the world I win release;
Nor scorn of men, nor footsteps rude,
Breaks in to mar the holy peace
Of this great solitude.

Kind nature to the aching heart
Brings sympathies of large relief:
Full gladly would she bear her part
In our dull load of grief.

So may the silent tears we weep
Lull the vexed spirit into rest,
As infants sob themselves to sleep
Upon a mother's breast.

But when the bitter hour is gone,
And the keen throbbing pangs are still,
Oh, sweetest then to couch alone
Upon some silent hill!

To live in joys that once have been,
To put the cold world out of sight;
And deck life's drear and barren scene
            With hues of rainbow light.

For what to man the gift of breath,
If sorrow be his lot below,
If all the day that ends in death
            Be dark with clouds of woe?

Shall the poor transport of an hour
Repay long years of sore distress?
The fragrance of a lonely flower
            Make glad the wilderness?

Ye golden hours of life's young spring,
Of innocence, of love and truth!
Bright beyond all imagining,
            Thou fairy dream of youth!

I'd give all wealth that toil hath piled,
The bitter fruit of life's decay,
To be once more a little child
            For one short sunny day.

THE PATH OF ROSES

THE PATH OF ROSES

IN the dark silence of an ancient room,
　Whose one tall window fronted to the West,

Where through laced tendrils of a hanging vine,
The sunset glow was fading into night,
Sat a pale Lady, resting weary hands
Upon a great clasped volume, and her face
Within her hands.
Not as in rest she bowed,
But large hot tears went coursing down her cheek,
And her low-panted sobs broke awfully
Upon the sleeping echoes of the night.
Soon she unclasped the volume once again,
And read the words in tone of agony,
As in self-torture, weeping as she read:

"He crowns the glory of his race;
He prayeth but in some fair place
To meet his foeman face to face;

"And battling for the true, the right,
From ruddy dawn to purple night,
To perish in the midmost fight;

"Where foes are fierce, and weapons strong
Where roars the battle loud and long,
Where blood is dropping in the throng.

"Still with a dim and glazing eye
To watch the tide of victory,
To hear in death the battle-cry.

"Then, gathered grandly to his grave,
To rest among the true and brave,

In holy ground, where yew-trees wave;
"Where, from church-windows sculptured fair,
Float out upon the evening air
The note of praise, the voice of prayer;

"Where no vain marble mockery
Insults with loud and boastful lie
The simple soldier's memory!

"Where sometimes little children go,
And read, in whispered accent low,
The name of him who sleeps below."

Her voice died out; like one in dreams she sat
"Alas!" she sighed, "for what can woman do?
Her life is aimless, and her death unknown;
Hemmed in by social forms she pines in vain:
Man has his work, but what can woman do?"
And answer came there from the creeping gloom,
The creeping gloom that settled into night:
"Peace, for thy lot is other than a man's;
His is a path of thorns; he beats them down—
He faces death—he wrestles with despair:
Thine is of roses; to adorn and cheer
His barren lot, and hide the thorns in flowers."
She spake again, in bitter tone she spake:
"Aye, as a toy, the puppet of an hour;
Or a fair posy, newly plucked at morn,
But flung aside and withered ere the night."
And answer came there from the creeping gloom,
The creeping gloom, that blackened into night:

"So shalt thou be the lamp to light his path,
What time the shades of sorrow close around."
And, so it seemed to her; an awful light
Pierced slowly through the darkness, orbed, and grew,
Until all passed away—the ancient room—
The sunlight dying through the trellised vine—
The one tall window—all had passed away
And she was standing on the mighty hills.
Beneath, around, as far as eye could see,
Squadron on squadron, stretched opposing hosts,
Ranked as for battle, mute and motionless.
Anon a distant thunder shook the ground,
The tramp of horses, and a troop shot by—
Plunged headlong in that living sea of men—
Plunged to their death: back from that fatal field
A scattered handful, fighting hard for life,
Broke through the serried lines, but as she gazed
They shrank and melted, and their forms grew thin—
Grew pale as ghosts when the first morning ray
Dawns from the east—the trumpet's brazen blare
Died into silence—and the vision passed;
Passed to a room where sick and dying lay,
In long, sad line—there brooded Fear and Pain—
Darkness was there, the shade of Azrael's wing.
But there was one that ever, to and fro,
Moved with light footfall : purely calm her face,
And those deep steadfast eyes that starred the gloom:
Still as she went, she ministered to each
Comfort and counsel; cooled the fevered brow
With softest touch, and in the listening ear
Of the pale sufferer whispered words of peace.

The dying warrior, gazing as she passed,
Clasped his thin hands and blessed her. Bless her too,
Thou who didst bless the merciful of old!
So prayed the Lady, as with tearful eyes
She watched her footsteps, till returning night
Had veiled her wholly, and the vision passed.
Then once again the awful whisper came:
"So in the darkest path of man's despair,
Where War and Terror shake the troubled earth,
Lies Woman's mission; with unblenching brow
To pass through scenes of horror and affright
Where men grow sick and tremble; unto her
All things are sanctified, for all are good.
Nothing so mean, but shall deserve her care;
Nothing so great, but she may bear her part.
No life is vain: each has his place assigned:
Do thou thy task, and leave the rest to heaven."
And there was silence, but the Lady made
No answer, save one deeply-breathed "Amen."
 And she arose, and in that darkening room
Stood lonely as a spirit of the night—
Stood calm and fearless in the gathered night—
And raised her eyes to heaven. There were tears
Upon her face, but in her heart was peace,
Peace that the world nor gives nor takes away!

THE THREE VOICES

THE THREE VOICES

The First Voice

With hands tight clenched through matted hair,
He crouched in trance of dumb despair
There came a breeze from out the air.

It passed athwart the gloomy flat—
It fanned his forehead as he sat—
It lightly bore away his hat,

All to the feet of one who stood
Like maid enchanted in a wood,
Frowning as darkly as she could.

With huge umbrella, lank and brown,
Unerringly she pinned it down,
Right through the centre of the crown.

Then, with an aspect cold and grim,
Regardless of its battered rim,
She took it up and gave it him.

Awhile like one in dreams he stood,
Then faltered forth his gratitude,
In words just short of being rude:

For it had lost its shape and shine,
And it had cost him four-and-nine,
And he was going out to dine.

With grave indifference to his speech,
Fixing her eyes upon the beach,
She said, "Each gives to more than each."

He raised his eyes in sudden awe,
And stammered out, "Thy wish is law!"
Yet knew not what he said it for.

"If that be so," she straight replied,
"Each heart with each doth coincide:
What boots it? for the world is wide."

And he, not wishing to appear
Less wise, said, "This Material Sphere
Is but Attributive Idea."

But when she asked him, "Wherefore so?"
He felt his very whiskers glow,
And frankly owned, "I do not know."

While, like broad waves of golden grain,
Or sunlit hues on cloistered pane,
His colour came and went again.

Pitying his obvious distress,
Yet with a tinge of bitterness,
She said, "The More exceeds the Less!"

"A truth of such undoubted weight,"
He urged, "and so extreme in date.
It were superfluous to state."

Roused into sudden passion, she
In tone of stern malignity:
"To others, yes; but not to thee."

Then proudly folded arm in arm:
But when he urged, "I meant no harm,"
Once more her speech grew mild and calm:

" Thought in the mind doth still abide,
That is by Intellect supplied,
And within that Idea doth hide.

"And he that yearns the truth to know,
Still further inwardly may go,
And find Idea from Notion flow.

"And thus the chain that sages sought
Is to a glorious circle wrought,
For Notion hath its source in Thought."

When he, with racked and whirling brain,
Feebly implored her to explain,
She simply said it all again.

Wrenched with an agony intense,
He spake, neglecting Sound and Sense,
And careless of all consequence:

"Mind—I believe—is Essence—Ent—
Abstract—that is—an Accident—
Which we—that is to say—I meant—"

When, with quick breath and cheeks all flushed,
At length his speech was somewhat hushed,
She looked at him, and he was crushed.

It needed not her calm reply,
She did the business with her eye,
And he could neither fight nor fly.

While she dissected, word by word,
His speech, half guessed at and half heard,
As might a cat a little bird.

Then, having wholly overthrown
His views, and stripped them to the bone,
Proceeded to unfold her own.

So passed they on with even pace,
Yet gradually one might trace
A shadow growing on his face.

THE SECOND VOICE

They walked beside the wave-worn beach,
Her tongue was very apt to teach,
And now and then he did beseech

She would abate her dulcet tone,
Because the talk was all her own,
And he was dull as any drone.

She urged, " No knife is like a fork,"
And ceaseless flowed her dreary talk,
Tuned to the footfall of a walk.

Her voice was very full and rich,
And when at length she asked him "Which?"
It mounted to its highest pitch.

He a bewildered answer gave,
Drowned in the sullen moaning wave,
Lost in the echoes of the cave.

He answered her he knew not what;
Like shaft from bow at random shot:
He spoke, but she regarded not.

She waited not for his reply,
But with a downward leaden eye,
Went on as if he were not by.

Sound argument and grave defence,
Strange questions raised on "why?" and "whence?"
And weighted down with common sense.

"Shall Man be Man? and shall he miss
Of other thoughts no thought but this,
Harmonious dews of sober bliss?

"What boots it? shall his fevered eye
Through towering nothingness descry
The grisly phantom hurry by?

"And hear dumb shrieks that fill the air;
See mouths that gape, and eyes that stare,
And redden in the dusky glare?

"The meadows breathing amber light,
The darkness toppling from the height,
The feathery train of granite Night?

"Shall he, grown gray among his peers,
Through the dark curtain of his tears,
Catch glimpses of his earlier years,

"And hear the sounds he knew of yore,
Old shufflings on the sanded floor,
Old footsteps kicking at the door?

"Yet still before him as he flies
One pallid form shall ever rise,
And, bodying forth in glassy eyes

"A dim reflex of vanished good,
Low peering through the tangled wood,
Shall freeze the current of his blood."

Still from each fact, with skill uncouth
And savage rapture, like a tooth
She wrenched some slow, reluctant truth.

Till, like some silent water-mill,
When summer suns have dried the rill,
She reached a full-stop, and was still.

Dead calm succeeded to the fuss,
As when the overladen bus
Has reached the railway terminus;

When for the tumult of the street,
Is heard the engines stifled beat,
The weary tread of porter's feet.

With glance that ever sought the ground,
She moved her lips without a sound,
And every now and then she frowned.

He gazed upon the sleeping sea,
And joyed in its tranquillity,
And in that silence dead, but she

To muse a little space did seem,
Then, like the echo of a dream,
Harped back upon her threadbare theme.

Still an attentive ear he lent,
But could not fathom what she meant:
She was not deep, nor eloquent.

He marked the ripple on the sand:
The even swaying of her hand
Was all that he could understand.

He left her, and he turned aside:
He sat and watched the coming tide,
Across the shores so newly dried.

He wondered at the waters clear,
The breeze that whispered in his ear,
The billows heaving far and near;

And why he had so long preferred
To hang upon her every word,
"In truth," he said, "it was absurd."

The Third Voice

NOT long this transport held its place,
Within a little moment's space
Quick tears were raining down his face.

His heart stood still, aghast with fear,
A wordless voice, nor far nor near,
He seemed to hear, and not to hear.

"Tears kindle not the doubtful spark:
If so; why not? Of this remark
The bearings are profoundly dark."

"Her speech," he said, "hath caused this pain
Easier I count it to explain
The jargon of the howling main.

"Or, stretched beside some sedgy brook,
To con, with inexpressive look,
An unintelligible book."

Low spake the voice within his head,
In words imagined more than said,
Soundless as ghost's intended tread:

"If thou art duller than before,
Why quittedst thou the voice of lore?
Why not endure, expecting more?"

"Rather than that," he groaned aghast,
"I'd writhe in depths of cavern vast,
Some loathly vampire's rich repast."

"'Twere hard," it answered, "themes immense
To coop within the narrow fence
That rings thy scant intelligence."

"Not so," he urged, "nor once alone:
But there was that within her tone
Which chilled me to the very bone.

"Her style was anything but clear,
And most unpleasantly severe;
Her epithets were very queer.

"And yet, so grand were her replies,
I could not choose but deem her wise,
I did not dare to criticise;

"Nor did I leave her, till she went
So deep in tangled argument
That all my powers of thought were spent."

A little whisper inly slid,
"Yet truth is truth : you know you did":
A little wink beneath the lid.

And sickening with excess of dread,
Prone to the dust he bent his head,
And lay like one three-quarters dead.

Forth went the whisper like a breeze;
Left him amid the wondering trees,
Left him by no means at his ease.

Once more he weltered in despair,
With hands through denser-matted hair
More tightly clenched than then they were.

When, bathed in dawn of living red,
Majestic frowned the mountain head,
"Tell me my fault," was all he said.

When, at high noon, the blazing sky
Scorched in his head each haggard eye,
Then keenest rose his weary cry.

And when at eve the unpitying Sun
Smiled grimly on the solemn fun,
"Alack," he sighed, "what have I done?"

But saddest, darkest was the sight,
When the cold grasp of leaden Night
Dashed him to earth and held him tight.

Tortured, unaided, and alone,
Thunders were silence to his groan,
Bagpipes sweet music to its tone:

"What? ever thus in dismal round,
Shall Pain and Mystery profound,
Pursue me like a sleepless hound,

"With crimson-dashed and eager jaws,
Me, still in ignorance of the cause,
Unknowing what I break of laws?"

The whisper to his ear did seem
Like echoed flow of silent stream,
Or shadow of forgotten dream;

The whisper trembling in the wind:
"Her fate with thine was intertwined,"
So spake it in his inner mind,

"Each orbed on each a baleful star,
Each proved the other's blight and bar,
Each unto each were best, most far:

"Yea, each to each was worse than foe,
Thou, a scared dullard, gibbering low,
And she, an avalanche of woe."

THE SAILORS WIFE

THE SAILORS WIFE

S EE! there are tears upon her face—
Tears newly shed and scarcely dried:
Close, in agonised embrace,
She clasps the infant at her side.

Peace dwells in those soft lidded eyes,
And parted lips that faintly smile;—
Peace, the foretaste of Paradise,
In heart too young for care or guile.

No peace that mother's features wear;
But quivering lips, and knotted brow,
And broken mutterings, all declare
The fearful dream that haunts her now.

The storm-wind, rushing through the sky,
Wails from the depths of cloudy space;
Shrill piercing as the seaman's cry
When death and he are face to face.

Familiar tones are in the gale,
They ring upon her startled ear,
And quick and low she pants the tale
That tells of agony and fear:

"Still that phantom-ship is nigh,—
With a vexed and life-like motion,
All beneath an angry sky,
Rocking on an angry ocean.

"Round the straining masts and shrouds
Throng the spirits of the storm;
Darkly seen through driving clouds,
Bends each gaunt and ghastly form.

"See! the good ship yields at last!
Dumbly yields and fights no more;
  Driving in the frantic blast,
  Headlong to the fatal shore.

"Hark! I hear her battered side,
  With a low and sullen shock,
  Dashed amid the foaming tide,
  Full upon a sunken rock.

"His face shines out against the sky,
  Like a ghost, so cold and white;
  With a dead despairing eye
Peering through the gathered night.

"Is he watching through the dark,
  Where a mocking ghostly hand
  Points, a faint and fickle spark,
Glimmering from the distant land?

"Sees he, in that hour of dread,
Hearth and home, and wife and child?
Loved ones who, in summers fled,
Clung to him, and wept and smiled?

"Reeling sinks the fated bark
  To her tomb beneath the wave;
  Must he perish in the dark—
Not a hand stretched out to save?

"See the spirits how they crowd!
Watching death with eyes that burn!
Waves rush in"—she shrieks aloud
   Ere her waking sense return.

The storm is gone: the skies are clear;
Hush'd is that bitter cry of pain:
The only sound that meets her ear
   The heaving of the sullen main.

For heaviness may 'dure a night,
But joy shall come with break of day;
She shudders with a strange delight;—
   The fearful dream is pass'd away.

She wakes; the grey dawn streaks the dark;
With early songs the copses ring;
Far off she hears the watch dog bark,
   A joyful bark of welcoming!

HIAWATHA'S PHOTOGRAPHING

HIAWATHA'S PHOTOGRAPHING

[*Introduction by the Author.*—In these days of imitation I can claim no sort of merit for this slight attempt at doing what is known to be so easy. Anyone who knows what verse is, with the smallest ear for rhythm, can throw off a composition in an easy running metre like The Song of Hiawatha. Having, then, made it quite clear that I challenge no attention in the following little poem to its merely verbal jingle, I must beg the candid reader to confine his criticism to its treatment of the subject.]

FROM his shoulder Hiawatha
    Took the camera of rosewood—
Made of sliding, folding rosewood—
Neatly put it all together.
    In its case it lay compactly,
Folded into nearly nothing;
But he opened out its hinges,
Pushed and pulled the joints and hinges
Till it looked all squares and oblongs,
Like a complicated figure
In the second book of Euclid.
    This he perched upon a tripod,
And the family, in order
Sat before him for their pictures—
Mystic, awful, was the process.
    First, a piece of glass he coated
With collodion, and plunged it
In a bath of lunar caustic

Carefully dissolved in water—
There he left it certain minutes.
    Secondly, my Hiawatha
Made with cunning hand a mixture
Of the acid pyrro-gallic,
And of glacial-acetic,
And of alcohol and water—
This developed all the picture.
    Finally, he fixed each picture
With a saturate solution
Which was made of hyposulphite,
Which, again, was made of soda.
(Very difficult the name is
For a metre like the present
But periphrasis has done it.)
    All the family, in order,
Sat before him for their pictures;
Each in turn, as he was taken,
Volunteered his own suggestions—
His invaluable suggestions.
    First, the governor—his father—
He suggested velvet curtains
Looped about a massy pillar,
And the corner of a table—
Of a rosewood dining table.
He would hold a scroll of something—
Hold it firmly in his left hand;
He would keep his right hand buried
(Like Napoleon) in his waistcoat;
He would gaze upon the distance—
(Like a poet seeing visions,

Like a man that plots a poem,
In a dressing gown of damask,
At 12.30 in the morning,
Ere the servants bring in luncheon)—
With a look of pensive meaning,
As of ducks that die in tempests.

    Grand, heroic was the notion:
Yet the picture failed entirely,
Failed because he moved a little—
Moved because he couldn't help it.

    Next his better half took courage—
She would have her picture taken:
She came dressed beyond description,
Dressed in jewels and in satin,
Far too gorgeous for an empress.
Gracefully she sat down sideways,
With a simper scarcely human,
Holding in her hand a nosegay
Rather larger than a cabbage.

    All the while that she was taking,
Still the lady chattered, chattered,
Like a monkey in the forest.
"Am I sitting still?" she asked him;
"Is my face enough in profile?
Shall I hold the nosegay higher?
Will it come into the picture?"
And the picture failed completely.

    Next the son, the stunning Cantab.,
He suggested curves of beauty,
Curves pervading all his figure,
Which the eye might follow onward

Till it centred in the breast-pin—
Centred in the golden breast-pin.
He Tad learnt it all from Ruskin,
(Author of *The Stones of Venice, Seven Lamps of Architecture, Modern Painters,* and some others)—
And perhaps he had not fully
Understood the author's meaning;
But, whatever was the reason,
All was fruitless, as the picture
Ended in a total failure..

    After him the eldest daughter:
She suggested very little,
Only begged she might be taken
With her book of "passive beauty."
Her idea of passive beauty
Was a squinting of the left eye,
Was a smile that went up sideways
To the corner of the nostrils.

    Hiawatha, when she asked him,
Took no notice of the question,
Looked as if he hadn't heard it;
But, when pointedly appealed to,
Smiled in a peculiar manner,
Coughed, and said it "didn't matter,"
Bit his lips, and changed the subject.

    Nor in this was he mistaken,
As the picture failed completely.

    So, in turn, the other daughters:
All of them agreed on one thing,
That their pictures came to nothing,
Though they differed in their causes,

From the eldest, Grinny-haha,
Who, throughout her time of taking,
Shook with sudden, ceaseless laughter,
With a silent fit of laughter,
To the youngest, Dinny-wawa,
Shook with sudden, causeless weeping—
Anything but silent weeping:
And their pictures failed completely
Last, the youngest son was taken:
"John" his Christian name had once been;
But his overbearing sisters
Called him names he disapproved of—
Called him Johnny, "Daddy's Darling"—
Called him Jacky, "Scrubby Schoolboy."
Very rough and thick his hair was,
Very dusty was his jacket,
Very fidgetty his manner,
And, so fearful was the picture,
In comparison the others
Might be thought to have succeeded—
To have partially succeeded—
    Finally, my Hiawatha
Tumbled all the tribe together
("Grouped" is not the right expression),
And, as happy chance would have it,
Did at last obtain a picture
Where the faces all succeeded:
Each came out a perfect likeness.
    Then they joined and all abused it—
Unrestrainedly abused it—
As "the worst and ugliest picture

That could possibly be taken
Giving one such strange expressions!
Sulkiness, conceit, and meanness!
Really any one would take us
(Any one who did not know us)
For the most unpleasant people!
(Hiawatha seemed to think so—
Seemed to think it not unlikely).
All together rang their voices—
Angry, hard, discordant voices—
As of dogs that howl in concert,
As of cats that wail in chorus.

   But my Hiawatha's patience,
His politeness, and his manners,
Unaccountably had vanished.
Not a minute more he waited,
But, to use his own expression,
His American expression,
Packed his traps, and "sloped for Texas,"
Neither did he leave them slowly,
With that calm deliberation—
That intense deliberation—
Which photographers aspire to,
But he left them in a hurry—
Left them in a mighty passion—
Stating that he would not stand it,
Stating, in emphatic language,
What he'd-be before he'd stand it.

NOVELTY AND ROMANCEMENT

NOVELTY AND ROMANCEMENT

A Broken Spell

I had grave doubts at first whether to call this passage of my life "A Wail," or "A Pæan," so much does it contain that is great and glorious, so much that is sombre and stern. Seeking for something which should be a sort of medium between the two, I decided, at last, on the above heading—wrongly, of course; I am always wrong: but let me be calm. It is a characteristic of the true orator never to yield to a burst of passion at the outset; the mildest of commonplaces are all he dare indulge in at first, and thence he mounts gradually;—"*vires acquirit eundo.*" (See cover.)* Suffice it, then, to say, in the first place, that I am *Leopold Edgar Stubbs*. I state this fact distinctly in commencing, to prevent all chance of the reader's confounding me either with the eminent shoe-maker of that name, of Pottle-street, Camberwell, or with my less reputable, but more widely known, namesake, Stubbs, the light comedian, of the Provinces; both which connexions I repel with horror and disdain: no offence, however, being intended to either of the individuals named—men whom I have never seen, whom I hope I never shall.

So much for commonplaces.

---

* The reader is referred to the title page of The Train reproduced early in this volume.—Ed.

Tell me now, oh! man, wise in interpretation of dreams and omens, how it chanced that, on a Friday afternoon, turning suddenly out of Great Wattles-street, I should come into sudden and disagreeable collision with an humble individual of unprepossessing exterior, but with an eye that glowed with all the fire of genius? I had dreamed at night that the great idea of my life was to be fulfilled. What was the great idea of my life? I will tell you. With shame and sorrow I will tell you.

My thirst and passion from boyhood (predominating over the love of taws and running neck and neck with my appetite for toffy) has been for poetry—for poetry in its widest and wildest sense—for poetry untrammelled by the laws of sense, rhyme, or rhythm, soaring through the universe, and echoing the music of the spheres! From my youth, nay, from my very cradle, I have yearned for poetry, for beauty, for novelty, for romancement. When I say "yearned," I employ a word mildly expressive of what may be considered as an outline of my feelings in my calmer moments: it is about as capable of picturing the headlong impetuosity of my life-long enthusiasm as those unanatomical paintings which adorn the outside of the Adelphi, representing Flexmore in one of the many conceivable attitudes into which the human frame has never yet been reduced, are of conveying to the speculative pit-goer a true idea of the feats performed by that extraordinary compound of humanity and Indian- rubber.

I have wandered from the point: that is a peculiarity, if I may be permitted to say so, incidental to life; and, as I remarked on an occasion which time will not suffer me more fully to specify, "What, after all, is life?" nor did I find any one of the individuals present (we were a party of nine, including the waiter, and it was while the soup was being removed that the above-recorded observation was made) capable of furnishing me with a rational answer to the question.

The verses which I wrote at an early period of life were eminently distinguished by perfect freedom from conventionalism, and were thus unsuited to the present exactions of literature: in a future age they will be read and admired, "when Milton," as my venerable uncle has frequently exclaimed, "when Milton and such like is forgot!" Had it not been for this sympathetic relative, I firmly believe that the poetry of my nature would never have come out; I can still recall the feelings which thrilled me when he offered me sixpence for a rhyme to "despotism." I never succeeded, it is true, in finding the rhyme, but it was on the very next Wednesday that I penned my well known *Sonnet on a Dead Kitten*, and in the course of a fortnight had commenced three epics, the titles of which I have unfortunately now forgotten.

Seven volumes of poetry have I given to an ungrateful world during my life; they have all shared the fate of true genius — obscurity and contempt. Not that any fault could be found with their contents; whatever their deficiencies may have been, *no reviewer has yet dared to criticise them.* This is a great fact.

The only composition of mine which has yet made any noise in the world, was a sonnet I addressed to one of the Corporation of Muggleton-cum-Swillside, on the occasion of his being elected Mayor of that town. It was largely circulated through private hands, and much talked of at the time; and though the subject of it, with characteristic vulgarity of mind, failed to appreciate the delicate compliments it involved, and indeed spoke of it rather disrespectfully than otherwise, I am inclined to think that it possesses all the elements of greatness. The concluding couplet was added at the suggestion of a friend, who assured me it was necessary to complete the sense, and in this point I deferred to his maturer judgement:—

> "When Desolation snatched her tearful prey
> From the lorn empire of despairing day;
> When all the light, by gemless fancy thrown,
> Served but to animate the putrid stone;
> When monarchs, lessening on the wildered sight,
> Crumblingly vanished into utter night;
> When murder stalked with thirstier stride abroad,
> And redly flashed the never-sated sword;
> In such an hour thy greatness had been seen—
> That is, if such an hour had ever been—
> In such an hour thy praises shall be sung,
> If not by mine, by many a worthier tongue;

And thou be gazed upon by wondering men,
When such an hour arrives, but not till then!"

Alfred Tennyson is Poet Laureate, and it is not for me to dispute his claim to that eminent position; still I cannot help thinking, that if the Government had only come forward candidly at the time, and thrown the thing open to general competition, proposing some subject to test the powers of the candidate (say *Frampton's Pill of Health, an Acrostic*), a very different result might have been arrived at.

But let us return to our muttons (as our noble allies do most unromantically express themselves), and to the mechanic of Great Wattles-street. He was coming out of a small shop—rudely built it was, dilapidated exceedingly, and in its general appearance seedy—what did I see in all this to inspire a belief that a great epoch in my existence had arrived? Reader, I saw the sign board!

Yes. Upon that rusty signboard, creaking awkwardly on its one hinge against the mouldering wall, was an inscription which thrilled me from head to foot with unwonted excitement. *Simon Lubkin. Dealer in Romance-ment.* Those were the very words.

It was Friday, the fourth of June, half-past four, p.m.

Three times I read that inscription through, and then took out my pocketbook, and copied it on the spot; the mechanic regarding me during the whole proceeding with a stare of serious and (as I thought at the time) respectful astonishment.

I stopped that mechanic, and entered into conversation with him : years of agony since then have gradually branded that scene upon my writhing heart, and I can repeat all that passed, word for word.

Did the mechanic (this was my first question) possess a kindred soul, or did he not?

Mechanic didn't know as he did.

Was he aware (this with thrilling emphasis) of the meaning of that glorious inscription upon his signboard?

Bless you, mechanic knew all about that 'ere.

Would mechanic (overlooking the suddenness of the invitation) object to adjourn to the neighbouring public-house, and there discuss the point more at leisure?

Mechanic would *not* object to a drain. On the contrary.

(Adjournment accordingly: brandy-and-water for two: conversation resumed.)

Did the article sell well, especially with the *"mobile vulgus"*?

Mechanic cast a look of good-natured pity on the questioner: the article sold well, he said, and the vulgars bought it most.

Why not add "Novelty" to the inscription? (This was a critical moment: I trembled as I asked the question.)

Not so bad an idea, mechanic thought: time was, it might have answered; but time flies, you see.

Was mechanic alone in his glory, or was there any one else who dealt as largely in the article?

Mechanic would pound it there was none.

What was the article employed for? (I brought this question out with a gasp, excitement almost choking my utterance.)

It would piece a'most anything together, mechanic believed, and make it solider nor stone.

This was a sentence difficult of interpretation. I thought it over a little, and then said, doubtfully, "you mean, I presume, that it serves to connect the broken threads of human destiny? to invest with a ——, with a sort of vital reality the chimerical products of a fertile imagination?".

Mechanic's answer was short, and anything but encouraging: "Mought be ———. I's no scollard, bless you."

At this point conversation certainly began to flag; I was seriously debating in my own mind whether this could really be the fulfilment of my life-cherished dream; so ill did the scene harmonise with my ideas of romance, and so painfully did I feel my companion's lack of sympathy in the enthusiasm of my nature — an enthusiasm which has found vent, ere now, in actions which the thoughtless crowd have too often attributed to mere eccentricity.

I have risen with the lark—"day's sweet harbinger"—(once, certainly, if not oftener), with the aid of a patent alarum, and have gone forth at that unseemly hour, much to the astonishment of the housemaid cleaning the door steps, to "brush with hasty steps the dewy lawn," and have witnessed the golden dawn with eyes yet half-closed in sleep (I have always stated to my friends, in any allusion to the subject, that my raptures at that moment were such that I have never since ventured to expose myself to the influence of excitement so dangerous. In confidence, however, I admit that the reality did not come up to the idea I had formed of it over night, and by no means repaid the struggle of getting out of bed so early).

I have wandered in the solemn woods at night, and bent me o'er the moss-grown fountain, to lave in its crystal stream my tangled locks and fevered brow. (What though I was laid up with a severe cold in consequence, and that my hair was out of curl for a week? Do paltry considerations such as these, I ask, affect the poetry of the incident?)

I have thrown open my small, but neatly furnished, cottage tenement, in the neighbourhood of St. John's Wood, and invited an aged beggar in to "sit by my fire, and talk the night away." (It was immediately after reading Goldsmith's *Deserted Village*. True it is that he told me nothing interesting, and that he took the hall-clock with him when he departed in the morning; still my uncle has always said that he wishes he had been there, and that it displayed in me a freshness and greenness of fancy (or "disposition," I forget which) such as he had never expected to see,)

I feel that it is incumbent on me to enter more fully into this latter topic—the personal history of my uncle: the world will one day learn to revere the talents of that wonderful man, though a want of funds prevents, at present, the publication of the great system of philosophy of which he is the inventor. Meanwhile, out of the mass of priceless manuscripts which he has bequeathed to an ungrateful nation, I will venture to select one striking specimen. And when the day arrives that my poetry is appreciated by the world at large (distant though it now appear!) then, I feel assured, shall his genius also receive its meed of fame!

Among the papers of that respected relative, I find what appears to have been a leaf torn from some philosophical work of the day: the following passage is scored. "Is this your rose? It is mine. It is yours. Are these your houses? They are mine. Give to me (of) the bread. She gave him a box on the ear." Against this occurs a marginal note in my uncle's hand writing; "some call this unconnected writing: I have my own opinion." This last was a favourite expression of his, veiling a profundity of ethical acumen on which it would be vain to speculate; indeed, so uniformly simple was the language of this great man, that no one besides myself ever suspected his possessing more than the ordinary share of human intellect.

May I, however, venture to express what I believe would have been my uncle's interpretation of this remarkable passage? It appears that the writer intended to distinguish the provinces of Poetry, Real Property, and Personal Property. The inquirer touches first on flowers, and with what a gush of generous feeling does the answer break upon him! "It is mine. It is yours." That is the beautiful, the true, the good; these are not hampered by petty considerations of "meum" and "tuum"; these are the common property of man. (It was with some such idea as this that I drew up the once celebrated bill, entitled *An Act for exempting Pheasants from the operation of the Game Laws, on the ground of Beauty*—a bill which would, doubtless, have passed both Houses in triumph, but that the member who had undertaken the care of it was unfortunately incarcerated in a Lunatic Asylum before it had reached the second reading). Encouraged by the success of his first question, our inquirer passes on to "houses" ("Real Property," you will observe); he is here met by the stern, chilling answer, "They are mine"—none of the liberal sentiment which dictated the former reply, but in its place a dignified assertion of the rights of property.

Had this been a genuine Socratic dialogue, and not merely a modern imitation, the inquirer would have probably here interrupted with "To me indeed," or, "I, for my part," or, "But how otherwise?" or some other of those singular expressions, with which Plato makes his characters display at once their blind acquiescence in their instructor's opinions, and their utter inability to express themselves grammatically. But the writer takes another line of thought; the bold inquirer, undeterred by the coldness of the last reply, proceeds from questions to demands, "give me (of) the bread"; and here the conversation abruptly ceases, but the moral of the whole is pointed in the narrative: "she gave him a box on the ear." This is not the philosophy of one individual or nation, the sentiment is, if I may so say, European; and I am borne out in this theory by the fact that the book has evidently been printed in three parallel columns, English, French, and German.

Such a man was my uncle ; and with such a man did I resolve to confront the suspected mechanic. I appointed the following morning for an interview, when I would personally inspect "the article" (I could not bring myself to utter the beloved word itself). I passed a restless and feverish night, crushed by a sense of the approaching crisis.

The hour came at last—the hour of misery and despair; it always does so, it cannot be put off for ever; even on a visit to a dentist, as my childhood can attest with bitter experience, we are not for ever getting there; the fatal door too surely dawns upon us, and our heart, which for the last half hour has been gradually sinking lower and lower and lower, until we almost doubt its existence, vanishes suddenly downwards into depths hitherto undreamed of. And so, I repeat it, the hour came at last.

Standing before that base mechanic's door, with a throbbing and expectant heart, my eye chanced to fall once more upon that signboard, once more I perused its strange inscription. Oh! fatal change! Oh! horror! What do I see? Have I been deluded by a heated imagination? A hideous gap yawns between the N and the C, making it not one word but two!

And the dream was over.

At the corner of the street I turned to take a sad fond look at the spectre of a phantom hope, I once had held so dear. "Adieu!" I whispered; this was all the last farewell I took, and I leant upon my walking-stick and wiped away a tear. On the following day I entered into commercial relations with the firm of Dumpy and

Spagg, wholesale dealers in the wine and spirit department.

The signboard yet creaks upon the mouldering wall, but its sound shall make music in these ears nevermore —ah! Nevermore.

Fig. 2: Simon Lubkin

SOME CARROLLEAN EPISODES CONCERNING TRAINS

" I thought of railway-travelling"

LEWIS CARROLL

SOME CARROLLEAN EPISODES CONCERNING TRAINS

Concerning the Toy Station in the Garden at Croft Rectory constructed by Lewis Carroll at the age of twelve.

Charles (Lewis Carroll) was at this time (c. 1844) very fond of inventing games for the amusement of his brothers and sisters; he constructed a rude train out of a wheelbarrow, a barrel and a small truck, which used to convey passengers from one " station " in the Rectory garden to another. At each of these stations there was a refreshment-room, and the passengers had to purchase tickets from him before they could enjoy their ride.

The Life and Letters of Lewis Carroll
by Stuart Dodgson Collingwood.

As (Alice) said these words her foot slipped, and in another moment, splash! she was up to her chin in salt water. Her first idea was that she had somehow fallen into the sea, "and in that case I can go back by railway," she said to herself. (Alice had been to the seaside once in her life, and had come to the general conclusion, that wherever you go to on the English coast you find a number of bathing machines in the sea, some children digging in the sand with wooden spades, the row of lodging houses, and behind them a railway station.)

Alice's Adventures in Wonderland, 1865.

"TICKETS, please!" said the Guard, putting his head in at the window. In a moment everybody was holding out a ticket: they were about the same size as the people, and quite seemed to fill the carriage.

"Now then! Show your ticket, child!" the Guard went on, looking angrily at Alice. And a great many voices all said together ("like the chorus of a song," thought Alice), "Don't keep him waiting, child! Why, his time is worth a thousand pounds a minute!"

"I'm afraid I haven't got one," Alice said in a frightened tone: "there wasn't a ticket-office where I came from." And again the chorus of voices went on. "There wasn't room for one where she came from. The land there is worth a thousand pounds an inch!"

"Don't make excuses," said the Guard: "you should have bought one from the engine-driver." And once more the chorus of voices went on with "The man that drives the engine. Why, the smoke alone is worth a thousand pounds a puff!" Alice thought to herself, "Then there's no use in speaking." The voices didn't join in this time, as she hadn't spoken, but, to her great surprise, they all thought in chorus (I hope you understand what thinking in chorus means—for I must confess that I don't), "Better say nothing at all. Language is worth a thousand pounds a word!"

"I shall dream about a thousand pounds tonight, I know I shall!" thought Alice.

All this time the Guard was looking at her, first through a telescope, then through a microscope, and then through an opera-glass. At last he said "You're travelling the wrong way," and shut up the window and went away.

"So young a child," said the gentleman sitting opposite to her, (he was dressed in white paper,) "ought to know which way she's going, even if she doesn't know her own name!"

A Goat, that was sitting next to the gentleman in white, shut his eyes and said in a loud voice, "She ought to know her way to the ticket-office, even if she doesn't know her alphabet!"

There was a Beetle sitting next the Goat (it was a very queer set of passengers altogether), and, as the rule seemed to be that they should all speak in turn, he went on with "She'll have to go back from here as luggage!"

Alice couldn't see who was sitting beyond the Beetle, but a hoarse voice spoke next. "Change engines ———" it said, and there it choked and was obliged to leave off.

"It sounds like a horse," Alice thought to herself. And an extremely small voice, close to her ear, said, "You might make a joke on that—something about 'horse' and 'hoarse,' you know."

"Then a very gentle voice in the distance said " She must be labelled 'Lass, with care,' you know ———"

And after that other voices went on ("What a number of people there are in the carriage!" thought Alice), saying "She must go by post, as she's got a head on her ——" "She must be sent as a message by the telegraph ——" "She must draw the train herself the rest of the way ——," and so on.

But the gentleman dressed in white paper leaned forwards and whispered in her ear, "Never mind what they all say, my dear, but take a return-ticket every time the train stops."

"Indeed I sha'n't!" Alice said rather impatiently. "I don't belong to this railway journey at all—I was in a wood just now—and I wish I could get back there!"
Through the Looking Glass, 1871.

Many of (Carroll's) friendships with children began in a railway carriage, for he always took about with him a stock of puzzles when he travelled, to amuse any little companions whom chance might send him. Once he was in a carriage with a lady and her little daughter, both complete strangers to him. The child was reading *Alice in Wonderland*, and when she put her book down, he began talking to her about it. The mother soon joined in the conversation, of course without the least idea who the stranger was with whom she was talking. "Isn't it sad," she said, "about poor Mr. Lewis Carroll? He's gone mad, you know." "Indeed," replied Mr. Dodgson, "I had never heard that." "Oh, I assure you it is quite true," the lady answered. "I have it on the best authority." Before Mr. Dodgson parted with her, he obtained her leave to send a present to the little girl, and a few days afterwards she received a copy of *Through the Looking-Glass*, inscribed with her name, and "From the Author, in memory of a pleasant journey."

G REAT were (Carroll's) preparations before going a journey; each separate article used to be carefully wrapped up in a piece of paper all to itself, so that his trunks contained nearly as much paper as of the more useful things. The bulk of the luggage was sent on a day or two before by goods train, while he himself followed on the appointed day, laden only with his well-known little black bag, which he always insisted on carrying himself.

Life and Letters

T hey threatened his life with a railway share

The Hunting of the Snark, 1876.

Y es, my Lady, change at Fayfield," were the next words I heard (oh that too obsequious Guard!), "next station but one." And the door closed, and the lady settled down into her corner, and the monotonous throb of the engine (making one feel as if the train were some gigantic monster, whose very circulation we could feel) proclaimed that we were once more speeding on our way...

"Fayfield Junction, my Lady, change for Elveston!" the Guard announced, flinging open the door of the carriage: and we soon found ourselves, with all our portable property around us, on the platform.

The accommodation, provided for passengers waiting at this Junction, was distinctly inadequate —— a single wooden bench, apparently intended for three sitters only: and even this was already partially occupied by a very old man, in a smock frock, who sat, with rounded shoulders and drooping head, and with hands clasped on the top of his stick so as to make a sort of pillow for that wrinkled face with its look of patient weariness.

"Come, you be off!" the Station-master roughly accosted the poor old man. "You be off, and make way for your betters! This way, my Lady!" he added in a perfectly different tone. "If your Ladyship will take a seat, the train will be up in a few minutes." The cringing servility of his manner was due, no doubt, to the address legible on the pile of luggage, which announced their owner to be "Lady Muriel Orme, passenger to Elveston, viâ Fayfield Junction."

As I watched the old man slowly rise to his feet, and hobble a few paces down the platform, the lines came to my lips:—

> *"From sackcloth couch the Monk arose,*
> *With toil his stiffen'd limbs he rear'd;*
> *A hundred years had flung their snows*
> *On his thin locks and floating beard."*

But the lady scarcely noticed the little incident. After one glance at the "banished man," who stood tremulously leaning on his stick, she turned to me. "This is *not* an American rocking-chair, by any means! Yet may I say," slightly changing her place, so as to make room for me beside her, "may I say, in Hamlet's words, 'Rest, rest——'" she broke off with a silvery laugh.

"'——perturbed Spirit!'" I finished the sentence for her. "Yes, that describes a railway-traveller *exactly!* And here is an instance of it," I added, as the tiny local train drew up alongside the platform, and the porters bustled about, opening carriage-doors—one of them helping the poor old man to hoist himself into a third-class carriage, while another of them obsequiously conducted the lady and myself into a first-class.

She paused, before following him, to watch the progress of the other passenger. "Poor old man!" she said. "How weak and ill he looks! It was a shame to let him be turned away like that. I'm very sorry——" At this moment it dawned on me that these words were not addressed to me, but that she was unconsciously thinking aloud. I moved away a few steps, and waited to follow her into the carriage, where I resumed the conversation.

"Shakespeare must have travelled by rail, if only in a dream: 'perturbed Spirit' is such a happy phrase."

"'Perturbed' referring, no doubt," she rejoined, "to the sensational booklets peculiar to the Rail. If Steam has done nothing else, it has at least added a whole new species to English Literature!"

"No doubt of it," I echoed. "The true origin of all our medical books—and all our cookery- books——"

"No, no!" she broke in merrily. "I didn't mean our Literature! We are quite abnormal. But the booklets—the little thrilling romances, where the Murder comes at page fifteen, and the Wedding at page forty—surely they are due to Steam?"

"And when we travel by Electricity—if I may venture to develop your theory—we shall have leaflets instead of booklets, and the Murder and the Wedding will come on the same page."

Sylvie and Bruno, 1889.

www.ingramcontent.com/pod-product-compliance
Lightning Source LLC
LaVergne TN
LVHW030411120526
838202LV00098BA/287